The Twelve Knits of Christmas

First published in the UK in 2011 by
Ivy Press
210 High Street
Lewes
East Sussex BN7 2NS
United Kingdom
www.ivypress.co.uk

British Library Cataloguing-in-Publication Data
A catalogue record for this book is available
from the British Library

ISBN: 978-1-907332-90-6

This book was conceived,
designed and produced by
Ivy Press
Creative Director *Peter Bridgewater*
Publisher *Jason Hook*
Editorial Director *Tom Kitch*
Senior Designer *James Lawrence*
Designer *Becky Herriott*
Photographer *Andrew Perris*
Illustrator *Debbie Powell*

Printed in China

Colour origination by Ivy Press Reprographics

10 9 8 7 6 5 4 3 2 1

The Twelve Knits of Christmas

Fiona Goble

Ivy Press

Contents

Introduction

Welcome to *The Twelve Knits of Christmas* – a delightful knitted version of the well-known Christmas song, 'The Twelve Days of Christmas'.

Inside, you'll find not just the song itself but also twelve easy-to-follow knitting patterns that will enable you to create all the woolly stars of this charming verse. There's also a colourful pear tree at the back of the book, which will provide the perfect perch for your knitted partridge.

'The Twelve Days of Christmas' is an English song which was first written down in the eighteenth century. But people were almost certainly singing it for many years before that. And perhaps not just in England – some people believe the song originated in France.

The twelve days in the song are the days between Christmas and a festival called the Epiphany, celebrated on 6 January each year. The festival marks the day when the three wise men arrived in Bethlehem to give Jesus their gifts.

The festival now marks the end of the Christmas celebrations and, in many countries, it's considered unlucky if you haven't packed away your Christmas decorations by this date.

Some people consider the song to be nothing more than a nonsense rhyme that is fun to sing, because it gradually builds up from a single unusual gift to a long list of twelve. Others think the verse was a secret way to teach children about Christianity and the Bible.

Whatever you think about the song, we hope you have a lovely time knitting all the characters. And don't forget – you don't have to stick to the colours we've chosen. If you want your dancing ladies in mint green or fancy a quartet of calling birds that are a touch more colourful, it's entirely up to you.

So rummage through your knitting stash, get out your needles and start knitting.

Everything you need

One of the best things about knitting is that you can do it pretty much anywhere and you don't need much to get started – just a ball of yarn and a pair of knitting needles. While these projects require a few things more, you've probably got most of them already. And if you haven't, you can easily get hold of them in your local craft or knitting shop.

Tension

The tension of a piece of knitting refers to the number of stitches and rows there are within a particular area of your knitting.

For these projects, we recommend that you knit a square of knitting to check your tension. The tension should be 12 stitches and 16 rows to a 4-cm (1½-in) square. If your knitting is a bit tight, try knitting on needles that are a size larger than recommended. If your knitting is a bit loose, choose needles that are a size smaller.

For these projects, tension is not as important as it is when you are knitting garments. But it is important that your knitted pieces are quite dense, otherwise you may find that the stuffing shows through and that your finished items do not keep their shape.

Yarn

Almost all the projects in this book are knitted with standard double knitting (DK) yarn.

We do not recommend any particular brand of yarn – browse through the shelves of your local knitting shop or your knitting stash to see which ones you like. You can also check out your local thrift shop or organize a yarn swap with friends or fellow knitters in your local knitting group or club.

The most important feature of the yarn is that it should be 100% wool or a mix of wool and acrylic. If you use 100% acrylic yarns or 100% cotton yarns, the results will be disappointing – even if the yarns themselves are good quality. This is because these yarns are less stretchy and a bit flat, which will make your finished projects look bulky and lumpy.

The only other yarn you will need to complete your twelve knits of Christmas is a small amount of gold crochet yarn for the five gold rings. This yarn is sold in most craft and knitting shops.

Each of the projects in this book includes the length and weight of the yarns you will need to complete the project. Because the exact quantity you will use will depend to some extent on the type and brand of yarn you use and the tension of your knitting, please use the figures as a guideline only.

Knitting needles

To make all the projects in this book you will need two pairs of knitting needles – one pair should be size 3 mm (US 2/3) and the other pair should be size 2.25 mm (US 1). We recommend short needles, because the projects are small and you will find shorter needles more manageable. It will be easier to get into the stitches if you can find needles with relatively sharp ends.

A crochet hook

You will need a 3.25 mm (US D-3) crochet hook for most of the projects in this book. There is no crochet involved as such, but some projects require simple crochet chains.

A yarn or tapestry needle

You will need a needle with an eye large enough to thread yarn through, and a fairly blunt end, to sew your knitting together.

An embroidery needle

You will need an embroidery needle to embroider the characters' features. Choose a needle with an eye large enough to thread through your yarn.

A standard sewing needle

You will need an ordinary needle for sewing buttons onto some of the dolls' clothing.

A water-soluble pen

These are like ordinary felt-tip pens but the ink disappears when it is dabbed with water. They are very useful for marking the position of some of the features on the birds and dolls before you embroider them. The pens are safe to use on almost all types of yarn, but it is worth testing on a spare, matching piece of yarn before you use them.

A red crayon

You will need an ordinary red crayon to add rosy cheeks to most of the human figures.

A pair of small scissors

A pair of scissors is required for trimming the yarn tails of your wool and trimming the yarns used for embroidering your finished projects.

Polyester toy filling

All the characters are stuffed with 100% polyester toy filling. This is a light, fluffy material that is specially made for filling toys and other hand-crafted items. You can buy it in sewing and craft shops and it's always worth checking that it conforms to safety standards.

A few buttons

A few of the projects require a small number of buttons. You may have them already or you can buy them in sewing and craft shops.

Ordinary sewing thread

You will need a small amount of ordinary sewing thread for sewing the buttons onto some of the dolls' clothes.

beg	beginning
cont	continue
inc1	increase one into the next stitch by knitting into the front and back of the stitch
K	knit
k2tog	knit the next 2 stitches together
kwise	by knitting the stitch(es)
m1	make one stitch (by picking up the horizontal loop lying before the next stitch and knitting into the back of it)
P	purl
p2tog	purl the next 2 stitches together
psso	pass slipped stitch over (pass the slipped stitch over the stitch just knitted)
pwise	by purling the stitch(es)
rem	remaining
rep	repeat
rs	right side
s1	slip one (slip a stitch onto your right-hand needle without knitting it)
ssk	slip, slip, knit (slip 2 stitches one at a time, then knit the 2 slipped stitches together)
st(s)	stitch(es)
st st	stocking (stockinette) stitch
ws	wrong side
yf	yarn forward (bring your yarn from the back to the front of your work)
cm	centimetre(s)
g	gram(s)
in	inch(es)
m	metre(s)
mm	millimetre(s)
oz	ounce(s)
yd(s)	yard(s)

The knack of knitting

If you've done any kind of knitting before, the projects in this book will be well within your grasp. All you need to know is how to cast on and cast off, how to work knit and purl stitches and how to increase and decrease the number of stitches on your needle. In case you need reminding, here's how it's all done.

Casting on
We recommend you use the cable method of casting on, which uses two needles.

1 Make a slip knot by making a loop in the yarn and drawing a loop of yarn through this loop. Put the slip knot onto one of your needles and pull on the yarn 'tail' quite firmly to tighten the slip knot on the needle. This is your first cast-on stitch.

2 Put the needle with the first cast-on stitch into your left hand. Now insert the tip of your other needle into the front of the stitch and under the left-hand needle. Wind the yarn (from the ball of yarn, not the yarn tail) around the tip of the right-hand needle.

3 Using the tip of the needle, draw the yarn through the slip knot to form a loop.

4 Now put the loop, which is your new stitch, onto the left-hand needle.

5 To make the next stitch, insert the tip of your right-hand needle between the two stitches on the left-hand needle. Wind the yarn over the right-hand needle, from left to right.

6 Just as in step 3, draw the yarn through the stitch to form a loop and transfer this loop to the right-hand needle.

> * Repeat steps 5 and 6 until you have cast on the right number of stitches for your project.

Making knit stitches
This is the basic knitting stitch. If you work every row in knit stitches, your knitted fabric is called garter stitch.

1 Holding the needle with the cast-on stitches in your left hand, insert the tip of your right-hand needle into the front of the first cast-on stitch.

2 Wind the yarn around the tip of your right-hand needle, from left to right.

3 With the tip of your right-hand needle, pull the yarn through the stitch to form a loop. This loop is your new stitch.

4 Slip the original stitch off your left-hand needle by gently pulling your right-hand needle to the right.

> * Repeat these steps until you have knitted all the stitches on your left-hand needle. To work the next row, transfer the needle with all the stitches into your left hand.

Making purl stitches

This is like working knit stitches backwards.
If you work alternate rows of knit and purl
stitches, your knitted fabric is called stocking or
stockinette stitch. The purl stitches are worked
on the reverse or 'wrong' side of your work
and the knit stitches on the front or 'right' side.

1 Holding the needle with the stitches in
your left hand, insert the tip of your
right-hand needle into the front of the
first stitch, from right to left.

2 Wind the yarn around the point of your
right-hand needle, from right to left.

3 With the tip of your needle, pull the yarn
through the stitch to form a loop. This
loop is your new stitch.

4 Slip the original stitch off your left-hand
needle by gently pulling your right-hand
needle to the right.

> ✳ Repeat these steps until you have
> purled all the stitches on your left-
> hand needle. To work the next row,
> transfer the needle with all the stitches
> into your left hand.

Casting off

In most cases, you will cast off knitwise, which means that you will knit the stitches before you
cast them off.

1 First, knit two stitches in the normal way.
Then, with the tip of your left-hand needle,
pick up the first stitch you knitted and lift
it over the second stitch.

2 The cast off stitch forms a flattened loop
across the top of the fabric. Continue by
knitting another stitch, so that you have
two stitches on your needle once more.

> ✳ Repeat these two steps until you have
> just a single stitch on your right-hand
> needle. Trim the yarn, leaving a yarn
> tail long enough to stitch your work
> together, and pull the tail all the way
> through the last stitch.

Casting off purlwise

In a few of the projects in this book, you will
need to cast off purlwise. This is exactly like
ordinary casting off, except that you purl the
stitches rather than knit them.

1 First, purl two stitches in the normal way.
Then, with the tip of your left-hand
needle, pick up the first stitch you purled
and lift it over the second stitch.

2 The cast off stitch forms a flattened loop
across the top of the fabric. Continue by
purling another stitch, so that you have
two stitches on your needle once more.

> ✳ Repeat these two steps until you have
> just a single stitch on your right-hand
> needle. Trim the yarn, leaving a yarn
> tail long enough to stitch your work
> together, and pull the tail all the way
> through the last stitch.

Shaping up

Most of the projects in this book involve a fair bit of shaping. This is done by decreasing and increasing the number of stitches on your needle as you knit your pieces. You will need to know two ways of increasing and a few ways of decreasing the number of stitches on your needle.

Increasing by making an additional stitch (m1)

1 To make a stitch, pick up the horizontal strand that runs between two stitches, using your right-hand needle.

2 Transfer the strand to your left hand needle by inserting your needle from right to left through the front of the picked-up strand. Knit through the back of the stitch.

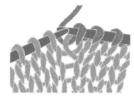

3 Transfer the new stitch to your right-hand needle.

Increasing by knitting into the next stitch twice (inc1)

Start by knitting your stitch in the normal way, but instead of slipping the old stitch off your needle, knit through the back of it before sliding it off. Remember that the instruction 'inc1' refers to both creating the additional stitch and knitting that stitch.

Decreasing by knitting two stitches together (k2tog)

Insert the point of your needle from left to right through the front of two stitches then knit them in the normal way.

Decreasing by purling two stitches together (p2tog)

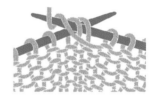

Insert the point of your needle from right to left through the front of two stitches then purl them in the normal way.

Decreasing by slipping 2 stitches, then knitting them together (ssk)

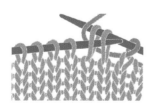

Insert the point of your right-hand needle into the first stitch from left to right and slip the stitch onto your right-hand needle without knitting it. Do the same with the next stitch. Then insert the left-hand needle through the front of both these stitches and knit them together.

Decreasing by slipping a stitch, knitting two stitches together and passing the slipped stitch over (s1, k2tog, psso)

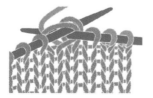

1 This is a way of decreasing two stitches at once. Insert the point of your right-hand needle into the first stitch from left to right and slip the stitch onto your right-hand needle without knitting it. Knit two stitches together.

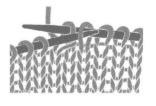

2 Using the point of your left-hand needle, lift the slipped stitch over the stitch in front.

All joined up

Watching your characters take shape as you sew your knitted pieces together is one of the most enjoyable parts of creating the birds and dolls in this book. But you have to be careful how you do it. Check out the recommended methods here and, if making small knitted items is new to you, remember that you may need a bit of practice to get the hang of it.

Mattress stitch

One version of this stitch is used to join vertical edges and another to join horizontal edges. It is worked from the right side of your work and the result is a seam that is very nearly invisible.

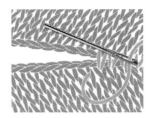

Vertical edges

With your two edges side by side, take your yarn under the running stitch between the first two stitches on one side. Then take the yarn under the corresponding running stitch between the first two stitches on the other side. Continue in this way, pulling your yarn up fairly tightly every few stitches.

Horizontal edges

With your two edges together, take your needle under the two 'legs' at the edge of one piece of knitting. Then take the yarn under the corresponding two 'legs' at the edge of the second piece of knitting. Continue in this way, pulling your yarn up fairly tightly every few stitches.

A version of mattress stitch can also be used to join some of the characters' limbs to their bodies and to close the gaps used for turning and stuffing.

Oversewing

This is a good method for joining small pieces or curved edges and is usually worked with the right sides of your pieces together. To work this stitch, take the yarn from the front over the edge of the seam and out through the front again.

Picking up stitches along an edge

Though this is not strictly a joining stitch, occasionally you will need to pick up stitches along an edge and knit onto these picked-up stitches.

A version of oversewing is also used to join some of the small pieces to the main part of your character – for example, some of the birds' beaks and feet.

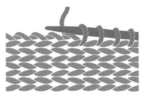

Vertical edge (the edges of a number of rows)

With the right side of your work facing you, insert your needle between the running threads of the first two stitches, then knit the stitch in the normal way.

Horizontal edge (cast-on or cast-off edges)

With the right side of your work facing you, insert your needle into the stitch of the last (or first) row and knit it in the normal way.

Other techniques

Facial features and hair are what give your dolls their individual character, so you need to know a few basic embroidery stitches and how to work a simple crochet chain. Another essential knitting technique is how to conceal yarn ends when your work is complete.

Crocheting a chain

While you do not need to be able to crochet to make the projects in this book, you do need to know how to make a simple crochet chain.

1 For the first link of the chain, make a slip knot on the crochet hook, in the same way as when beginning to cast on a piece of knitting. Holding the slip stitch on the hook, wind the yarn around the hook from the back to the front and catch the yarn in the crochet hook tip.

2 Pull the yarn through the loop on your hook to make the second stitch of the crochet chain.

❋ *Continue in this way until the chain is the desired length.*

Simple embroidery stitches

There are literally hundreds of embroidery stitches, but knowing just a few of the simplest ones will enable you to add facial features to your dolls.

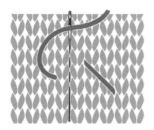

Straight stitch

This stitch is used to make the dolls' mouths and some of the bird markings. It is the simplest of all stitches and involves bringing the needle out on the front of the work at the point where you want the stitch to start and inserting it back at the point where you want the stitch to end.

French knots

These are used for the pupils of the birds' and dolls' eyes.

Bring the yarn out at the point where you want to work the stitch. With the needle close to the surface of your knitting, wind the yarn twice around the needle (or once only if you want the pupils a little smaller). Then insert the tip of your needle back into your knitting, just to the side of your starting point, and pull it all the way through; you may find it helpful to hold the wrapped yarn in place with your thumbnail as you do so. Bring the needle out at the starting point for the next French knot; if you are only working one French knot, take the needle to an inconspicuous area where you can then conceal it (see page 15).

Remember to work French knots between the strands of yarn rather than between stitches, otherwise you will find that the knots slip through your knitting.

Chain stitch

This stitch is used, among other things, for the irises of the eyes and some of the dolls' noses and hair.

Bring the needle out at the point where you want the stitch to start. Then insert the needle back into the knitting, just to the side of the starting point, and bring it out again a stitch length along, making sure that the needle tip lies over the little loop of yarn that you have formed. Now pull your yarn up fairly tightly so that the stitch is firm – but don't overdo it or your knitting will pucker.

Lace stitch and picot edging

Some projects use a simple technique to produce stitches and holes that form a lace pattern. Sometimes the lace is folded to form a wavy or 'picot' edge. The technique involves bringing the yarn to the front of the work and knitting two stitches together on the right side.

1 Bring your yarn from the back to the front of your work, under the right-hand needle.

2 Knit the next two stitches together, taking the yarn over the top of your needle.

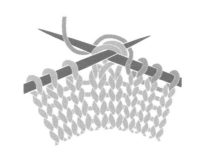

Starting and finishing your embroidery stitches

To start off, tie a simple knot or double knot at the end of the yarn. Insert the needle between stitches in an inconspicuous area on the back of your work and bring it out at the starting point. Pull your yarn quite firmly, so that the knot slips between the stitches and is embedded somewhere in the middle of your work.

When you have finished embroidering, take your needle out to an inconspicuous area on the back of your work. To secure the yarn, work a couple of very small stitches, one on top of the other, in the running stitches between the knitted stitches (these will be slightly sunken). Then conceal the yarn tail in the manner described to the right.

Concealing yarn ends

When you have finished your knitting and sewn your items together, you will usually have some loose yarn tails that need concealing. On a stuffed character, you can simply use your needle to thread the yarn tail into the body at the base of the yarn tail and out at another point. Then, squash the body slightly and trim the yarn tail close to the knitting. When the body springs back into shape, the yarn tail will disappear inside the character.

In the case of some of the characters' clothes and the gold rings, you will need to conceal the yarn tails by working a few running stitches forwards and then backwards in the garment's seam. It is a good idea to use your embroidery needle to do this and take the yarn tail between the strands of your yarn, as this will help it stay in position.

Reshaping finished pieces

Sometimes when you have finished your knitting, the item is not quite the shape you want. You will probably notice this more with the dolls' clothes than with items that are stuffed. If this is the case, simply soak the item in lukewarm water and squeeze out the excess. Reshape the item while it is damp and leave it to dry.

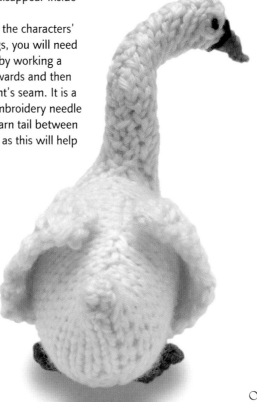

A partridge

He's the first gift to be offered and the least extravagant, but the partridge is the most famous character in the entire 'Twelve Days of Christmas' song. And with his pear tree perch, he's a regular on cards that celebrate the festive season. No doubt the original partridge was destined for the cooking pot. This one won't taste as good – but he promises to look as cute as pie and to stick around for ages.

Equipment

* A pair of size 3 mm (US 2/3) knitting needles
* A 3.25 mm (US D-3) crochet hook
* A needle to sew your work together
* An embroidery needle

For the partridge, you will need

* 4 g/⅛ oz (11 m/12 yds) flecked grey DK yarn
* Small amounts of orange and dark brown DK yarns
* Very small amounts of cream and black DK yarns
* 5 g (⅛–¼ oz) polyester toy filling

Body

Side 1

Make 1

* Cast on 6 sts in flecked grey.
* 1st row: K.
* Next and every ws row unless stated: P.
* Next rs row: K1, (inc1) 4 times, K1. [10 sts]
* Next rs row: K1, (inc1) twice, K4, (inc1) twice, K1. [14 sts]
* Next rs row: K1, (inc1) twice, K8, (inc1) twice, K1. [18 sts]
* Next rs row: K.
* Next row: Cast on 4 sts, P to end. [22 sts]
* Next row: K to last 3 sts, k2tog, K1. [21 sts]
* Next row: P.
* Rep last 2 rows twice more. [19 sts]
* Next row: K1, ssk, K to last 3 sts, k2tog, K1. [17 sts]
* Next rs row: K1, (ssk) twice, K7, (k2tog) twice, K1. [13 sts]
* Next rs row: K1, (ssk) twice, K3, (k2tog) twice, K1. [9 sts]
* Next row: p2tog, P5, p2tog. [7 sts]
* Next row: K1, ssk, K1, k2tog, K1. [5 sts]
* Cast off pwise.

Side 2

Make 1

* Cast on 6 sts in flecked grey.
* 1st row: K.
* Next and every ws row unless stated: P.
* Next rs row: K1, (inc1) 4 times, K1. [10 sts]
* Next rs row: K1, (inc1) twice, K4, (inc1) twice, K1. [14 sts]
* Next rs row: K1, (inc1) twice, K8, (inc1) twice, K1. [18 sts]
* Next row: Cast on 4 sts, K to end. [22 sts]
* Next rs row: K1, ssk, K to end. [21 sts]
* Next row: P.
* Rep last 2 rows twice more. [19 sts]
* Next row: K1, ssk, K to last 3 sts, k2tog, K1. [17 sts]
* Next rs row: K1, (ssk) twice, K7, (k2tog) twice, K1. [13 sts]
* Next rs row: K1, (ssk) twice, K3, (k2tog) twice, K1. [9 sts]
* Next row: p2tog, P5, p2tog. [7 sts]
* Next row: K1, ssk, K1, k2tog, K1. [5 sts]
* Cast off pwise.

Head

Make 1

* Cast on 12 sts in orange.
* Work 4 rows in st st, beg with a K row.
* Next row: (ssk) 3 times, (k2tog) 3 times. [6 sts]
* Cast off pwise.

Beak

Make 1

* Using your crochet hook and dark brown yarn, make a 1-cm (⅜-in) crochet chain.

Making up & finishing

Place the two body pieces right sides together and oversew around the edge, leaving a gap at the base for turning and stuffing. Turn the body right side out, stuff and stitch the gap closed.

Fold the head piece in half with the right sides together and oversew around the curved edge, leaving the flat side (where you cast on your stitches) open. Turn the head right side out and stuff it. Oversew the head in place on the body with the seam at the back.

Using dark brown yarn, work the outline of the wings in chain stitch.

Using black yarn, work two French knots for the eyes. Using cream yarn, work a circle of chain stitch around the eyes.

For the beak, fold the crochet chain in half widthways and secure it with a couple of running stitches. Use the yarn tails to stitch the beak to the head.

Using the flecked grey yarn, work two or three rows of chain stitches up the back of the head, from the nape of the neck to a point just before the beak.

On the second day of Christmas, my true love gave to me

Two turtle doves

And a partridge in a pear tree

Two turtle doves

Pretty little turtle doves were often kept as pets in cages during times gone by and were a symbol of love and peace. Most of the ornithological gifts in 'The Twelve Days of Christmas' were destined for the dining-room table, but this cute little pair were almost certainly an invitation to love and marriage.

Equipment
* A pair of size 3 mm (US 2/3) knitting needles
* A 3.25 mm (US D-3) crochet hook
* A needle to sew your work together
* An embroidery needle

For each turtle dove, you will need
* 4 g/⅛ oz (10 m/11 yds) mid-grey DK yarn
* A small amount of dark beige DK yarn
* Very small amounts of cream, black and dark brown DK yarns
* 5 g (⅛–¼ oz) polyester toy filling

Body & head
The body and head are worked as one piece.

Side 1
Make 1
* Cast on 4 sts in mid-grey.
* 1st row: (inc1, K1) twice. [6 sts]
* Next and every ws row unless stated: P.
* Next rs row: (inc1) twice, K1, (inc1) twice, K1. [10 sts]
* Next rs row: (inc1) twice, K to last 3 sts, (inc1) twice, K1. [14 sts]
* Next rs row: inc1, K to last 2 sts, inc1, K1. [16 sts]
* Next rs row: Cast on 6 sts, K to end. [22 sts]
* Next row: P to last 2 sts, p2tog. [21 sts]
* Next row: Cast off 2 sts, K to end. [19 sts]
* Next row: P to last 2 sts, p2tog. [18 sts]
* Next row: Cast off 4 sts, K to end. [14 sts]
* Next row: P to last 2 sts, p2tog. [13 sts]
* Next row: Cast off 4 sts, K to end. [9 sts]
* Next row: P to last 2 sts, p2tog. [8 sts]
* Next row: K.
* Next row: P to last 2 sts, p2tog. [7 sts]
* Work 3 rows in st st beg, with a K row.
* Next row: p2tog, P3, p2tog. [5 sts]
* Cast off.

Side 2
Make 1
* Cast on 4 sts in mid-grey.
* 1st row: (inc1, K1) twice. [6 sts]
* Next and every ws row unless stated: P.
* Next rs row: (inc1) twice, K1, (inc1) twice, K1. [10 sts]
* Next rs row: (inc1) twice, K to last 3 sts, (inc1) twice, K1. [14 sts]
* Next rs row: inc1, K to last 2 sts, inc1, K1. [16 sts]
* Next row: Cast on 6 sts pwise, P to end. [22 sts]
* Next row: K to last 2 sts, ssk. [21 sts]
* Next row: Cast off 2 sts pwise, P to end. [19 sts]
* Next row: K to last 2 sts, ssk. [18 sts]
* Next row: Cast off 4 sts pwise, P to end. [14 sts]

* Next row: K to last 2 sts, ssk. [13 sts]
* Next row: Cast off 4 sts pwise, P to end. [9 sts]
* Next row: K to last 2 sts, ssk. [8 sts]
* Next row: P.
* Next row: K to last 2 sts, ssk. [7 sts]
* Work 3 rows in st st, beg with a P row.
* Next row: k2tog, K3, ssk. [5 sts]
* Cast off pwise.

Wings

Right wing

Make 1

* Cast on 3 sts in dark beige.
* 1st row: (inc1) twice, K1. [5 sts]
* Next row: P.
* Next row: inc1, K2, inc1, K1. [7 sts]
* Work 5 rows in st st, beg with a P row.
* Next row: K to last 3 sts, ssk, K1. [6 sts]
* Next row: P.
* Rep last 2 rows 3 times more. [3 sts]
* Next row: ssk, K1. [2 sts]
* Next row: p2tog, break yarn and pull it through rem st.

Left wing

Make 1

* Cast on 3 sts in dark beige.
* 1st row: (inc1) twice, K1. [5 sts]
* Next row: P.
* Next row: inc1, K2, inc1, K1. [7 sts]
* Work 5 rows in st st, beg with a P row.
* Next row: K1, k2tog, K to end. [6 sts]
* Next row: P.
* Rep last 2 rows 3 times more. [3 sts]
* Next row: K1, k2tog. [2 sts]
* Next row: p2tog, break yarn and pull it through rem st.

Beak

* Using your crochet hook and dark brown yarn, make a 1-cm (³⁄₈-in) crochet chain.

Making up & finishing

Place the two body pieces right sides together and oversew around the edge, leaving a gap at the base of the body for turning and stuffing. Turn the body right side out. Stuff the body and stitch the gap closed.

Secure the wings by oversewing around the curved part, where the wings join the body – the ends of the wings should be free.

Using black yarn, work two French knots for the eyes. Using cream yarn, work a circle of chain stitch around the eyes.

For the beak, fold the crochet chain in half widthways and secure it with a couple of running stitches. Use the yarn tails to stitch the beak to the head.

On the third day of Christmas, my true love gave to me

Three French hens

Two turtle doves

And a partridge in a pear tree

Three French hens

No one seems quite sure why the hens in this Christmas song are French – although it may be that the song itself originated in France. The non-woolly relatives of this colourful trio were useful for their eggs and feathers as well as for their meat, so would have been a great present to receive. And while these hens are not exactly useful, we think they would make a great gift, too.

For each French hen, you will need

* 6 g/¼ oz (16 m/17 yds) flecked rust DK yarn
* Small amounts of red and orange DK yarns
* Very small amounts of yellow, black and white DK yarns
* 7 g (¼ oz) polyester toy filling

Body & head

The body and head are worked as one piece.

Side 1

Make 1

* Cast on 6 sts in flecked rust.
* 1st row: inc1, K3, inc1, K1. [8 sts]
* Next row: P.
* Next row: (inc1) twice, K to last 3 sts, (inc1) twice, K1. [12 sts]
* Next row: P.
* Rep last 2 rows once more. [16 sts]
* Work 2 rows in st st, beg with a K row.
* Next row: inc1, K to end. [17 sts]
* Next row: P.
* Rep last 2 rows twice more. [19 sts]
* Next row: K1, k2tog, K to end. [18 sts]
* Next row: P.
* Rep last 2 rows once more. [17 sts]
* Next row: Cast off 7 sts, K to end. [10 sts]
* Next row: P.
* Next row: K1, k2tog, K to end. [9 sts]
* Next row: P.
* Rep last 2 rows twice more. [7 sts]
* Next row: K1, k2tog, K1, ssk, K1. [5 sts]
* Work 3 rows in st st, beg with a P row.
* Next row: K2tog, K1, ssk. [3 sts]
* Cast off pwise.

Side 2

Make 1

* Cast on 6 sts in flecked rust.
* 1st row: inc1, K3, inc1, K1. [8 sts]
* Next row: P.
* Next row: (inc1) twice, K to last 3 sts, (inc1) twice, K1. [12 sts]
* Next row: P.
* Rep last 2 rows once more. [16 sts]
* Work 2 rows in st st, beg with a K row.
* Next row: K to last 2 sts, inc1, K1. [17 sts]
* Next row: P.
* Rep last 2 rows twice more. [19 sts]
* Next row: K to last 3 sts, ssk, K1. [18 sts]
* Next row: P.
* Next row: K to last 3 sts, ssk, K1. [17 sts]
* Next row: Cast off 7 sts pwise, P to end. [10 sts]
* Work 2 rows in st st, beg with a K row.
* Next row: K to last 3 sts, ssk, K1. [9 sts]
* Next row: P.
* Rep last 2 rows twice more. [7 sts]
* Next row: K1, k2tog, K1, ssk, K1. [5 sts]
* Work 3 rows in st st, beg with a P row.
* Next row: K2tog, K1, ssk. [3 sts]
* Cast off pwise.

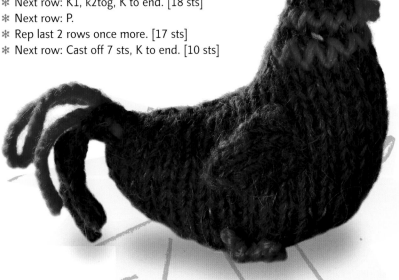

Wings

Make 2

* Cast on 5 sts in flecked rust.
* Work 6 rows in st st, beg with a K row.
* Next row: k2tog, K1, ssk. [3 sts]
* Next row: P.
* Next row: s1, k2tog, psso, break yarn and pull it through rem st.

Tail feathers

* Using your crochet hook, make two 9-cm (3½-in) crochet chains in flecked rust yarn and two 9-cm (3½-in) crochet chains in red yarn.

Claws

Make 2

Using your crochet hook and orange yarn, make a 2.5-cm (1-in) crochet chain, leaving long tails. Thread one tail back down the chain to the centre point. Insert your crochet hook into the middle stitch of the chain and, using the threaded-down yarn tail, make a 1.5-cm (½-in) chain from the centre to form the hen's middle claw. Thread the yarn tails down to the heel so that they can be used to secure the claw in place.

Comb

* Separate a length of red yarn into two thinner lengths.
* Using size 2.25 mm (US 1) needles and a thin length of red yarn, cast on 6 sts.
* 1st row: Cast off 3 sts, K to end.
* Next row: K.
* Next row: Cast on 3 sts, cast off 3 sts, K to end.
* Rep last 2 rows once more.
* Cast off.

Beak

* Using size 2.25 mm (US 1) needles, cast on 5 sts in yellow.
* Cast off.

Making up & finishing

Fold the beak in half widthways and oversew the edges together. Seam around the hen's head using mattress stitch, positioning and securing the comb and beak as you go. Seam around the body of the hen, using mattress stitch for the straight edges and oversewing the curves. Leave a gap at the bottom for stuffing. Stuff the hen and sew the gap closed.

Oversew the claws to the underside of the hen.

Secure the wings by oversewing the front part of the wing to the body – the outer edges of the wings should be free.

Using black yarn, work two French knots for the eyes. Split a short length of white yarn into two thinner lengths and use these to work a circle of chain stitch around the eyes.

Fold each tail feather crochet chain in half and use the yarn tails to fasten the tail feathers to the body.

For the neck feathers, use red yarn to work two rows of V-shaped stitches around the hen's neck. Use the same yarn to make two small loops below the beak for the hen's wattles.

On the fourth day of Christmas,

my true love gave to me

Four calling birds

Three French hens

Two turtle doves

And a partridge in a pear tree

Four calling birds

The four calling birds should really be four 'colly' or 'collie' birds, which is an old English name for blackbirds. Blackbirds were a cheap and tasty addition to the cooking pot – and another Christmas gift for food-lovers. They also make an appearance on the menu in the traditional English nursery rhyme, 'Sing a Song of Sixpence'.

Equipment

* A pair of size 3 mm (US 2/3) knitting needles
* A 3.25 mm (US D-3) crochet hook
* A needle to sew your work together
* An embroidery needle

For each calling bird, you will need

* 3 g/⅛ oz (9 m/10 yds) black DK yarn
* A very small amount of bright yellow DK yarn
* 4 g (⅛ oz) polyester toy filling

Body & head

The body and head are knitted as one piece.

Side 1

Make 1
* Cast on 4 sts in black.
* 1st row: (inc1, K1) twice. [6 sts]
* Next row: P.
* Next row: (inc1) twice, K1, (inc1) twice, K1. [10 sts]
* Next row: P.
* Next row: (inc1) twice, K5, (inc1) twice, K1. [14 sts]
* Work 5 rows in st st, beg with a P row.
* Next row: Cast on 5 sts, K to end. [19 sts]
* Next row: P.
* Next row: Cast off 12 sts, K to end. [7 sts]
* Work 4 rows in st st, beg with a P row.
* Next row: p2tog, P3, p2tog. [5 sts]
* Next row: k2tog, K1, ssk. [3 sts]
* Cast off pwise.

Side 2

Make 1
* Cast on 4 sts in black.
* 1st row: (inc1, K1) twice. [6 sts]
* Next row: P.
* Next row: (inc1) twice, K1, (inc1) twice, K1. [10 sts]
* Next row: P.
* Next row: (inc1) twice, K5, (inc1) twice, K1. [14 sts]
* Work 4 rows in st st, beg with a P row.
* Next row: Cast on 5 sts, P to end. [19 sts]
* Next row: K.
* Next row: Cast off 12 sts pwise, P to end. [7 sts]
* Work 4 rows in st st, beg with a K row.
* Next row: k2tog, K3, ssk. [5 sts]
* Next row: p2tog, K1, p2tog. [3 sts]
* Cast off.

Wings

The two wings are knitted as one piece.

Make 1

* Cast on 6 sts in black.
* 1st row: inc1, K3, inc1, K1. [8 sts]
* Next row: P.
* Next row: inc1, K5, inc1, K1. [10 sts]
* Next row: P.
* Next row: K5, turn and work on these 5 sts only.
* Work 2 rows in st st, beg with a P row.
* Next row: p2tog, P3. [4 sts]
* Next row: K.
* Next row: p2tog, P2. [3 sts]
* Next row: K.
* Next row: p2tog, P1. [2 sts]
* Next row: K.
* Next row: p2tog, break yarn and pull it through rem st.

* Join yarn to rem sts on rs of work.
* Next row: K.
* Work 2 rows in st st, beg with a P row.
* Next row: P3, p2tog. [4 sts]
* Next row: K.
* Next row: P2, p2tog. [3 sts]
* Next row: K.
* Next row: P1, p2tog. [2 sts]
* Next row: K.
* Next row: p2tog, break yarn and pull it through rem st.

Beak

Using your crochet hook and bright yellow yarn, make a 1-cm (⅜-in) crochet chain.

Making up & finishing

Place the two body pieces right sides together and oversew around the edge, leaving a gap at the top of the body for turning and stuffing. Turn the body right side out. Stuff the main body fairly lightly, but do not stuff the tail part. Close the gap.

Oversew the top part of the wings in place at the neck edge of the bird.

Divide a length of bright yellow yarn into two thinner strands. Use one of these to work a small circle of yellow chain stitch on each side of the head for the eyes. Using black yarn, work a French knot in the centre of each chain stitch circle.

Thread the yarn tails to the centre of the crochet chain for the beak and use these to sew the beak in place.

On the fifth day of Christmas, my true love gave to me

Five gold rings

Four calling birds

Three French hens

Two turtle doves

And a partridge in a pear tree

Five gold rings

Most people assume that in this verse the carol-singer is telling us about her beloved's gift of precious jewels. But historians beg to differ. Apparently, the five gold rings referred to ring-necked pheasants, which were hunted and eaten by only the very noblest of citizens. We've stuck to non-bird versions of gold rings here, however – and you should be able to slip them onto the average finger.

Equipment

* A pair of size 3 mm (US 2/3) knitting needles
* A needle to sew your work together
* An embroidery needle

For five rings and the cushion, you will need

* A small amount of gold crochet yarn
* 6 g/¼ oz (17 m/19 yds) dark red DK yarn
* A small amount of bright pink DK yarn
* 7 g (¼ oz) polyester toy filling

Rings

Make 5
* Cast on 22 sts in gold crochet yarn.
* K 1 row.
* Cast off.

Mini cushion

Front

Make 1
* Cast on 19 sts in dark red.
* K 4 rows.
* Next row: K.
* Next row: K3, P13, K3.
* Next row: K9, join bright pink yarn and K1, pick up red yarn and K to end.
* Next row: (K3, P5) red, P3 pink, (P5, K3) red.
* Next row: K8 red, K3 pink, K8 red.
* Next row: (K3, P4) red, P5 pink, (P4, K3) red.
* Next row: K7 red, K5 pink, K7 red.
* Next row: (K3, P3) red, P7 pink, (P3, K3) red.
* Next row: K6 red, K7 pink, K6 red.
* Next row: (K3, P3) red, P7 pink, (P3, K3).
* Next row: K6 red, K3 pink, K1 red, K3 pink, K6 red.

Making up & finishing

Join the short edges of the five gold knitted strips to form rings.

Using bright pink yarn, work chain stitch around the edges of the heart (optional). Seam the cushion pieces together using mattress stitch, leaving a gap open for stuffing. Stuff fairly lightly and stitch the gap closed.

* Next row: (K3, P4) red, P1 pink, P3 red, P1 pink, (P4, K3) red. Break pink yarn.
* Next row: K.
* Next row: K3, P13, K3.
* Rep last 2 rows once more.
* K 4 rows.
* Cast off.

Back

Make 1
* Cast on 19 sts in dark red.
* K 4 rows.
* Next row: K.
* Next row: K3, P13, K3.
* Rep last 2 rows 7 times more.
* K 4 rows.
* Cast off.

On the sixth day of Christmas, my true love gave to me

Six geese a-laying

Five gold rings

Four calling birds

Three French hens

Two turtle doves

And a partridge in a pear tree

Six geese a-laying

Geese were among the first types of fowl to be domesticated – captured and kept for egg laying and breeding rather than just for meat. Luckier than most of the song's cast of birds, these geese were gifted for their egg-laying skills rather than their flavour when roasted. Although these little woolly cousins are a little different, we think they would make an equally lovely Christmas offering.

Equipment

* **A pair of size 3 mm (US 2/3) knitting needles**
* **A needle to sew your work together**
* **An embroidery needle**

For each goose, you will need

* 5 g/⅛–¼ oz (13 m/14 yds) flecked grey DK yarn
* Small amounts of mid-grey and orange DK yarns
* Very small amounts of cream and black DK yarns
* 7 g (¼ oz) polyester toy filling

Body & head
The body and head are knitted as one piece.

Side 1
Make 1
* Cast on 6 sts in flecked grey.
* 1st row: inc1, K3, inc1, K1. [8 sts]
* Next row: P.
* Next row: (inc1) twice, K to last 3 sts, (inc1) twice, K1. [12 sts]
* Next row: P.
* Rep last 2 rows once more. [16 sts]
* Work 2 rows in st st, beg with a K row.
* Next row: K to last 2 sts, inc1, K1. [17 sts]
* Next row: P.
* Rep last 2 rows once more. [18 sts]
* Next row: K to last 2 sts, inc1, K1. [19 sts]
* Next row: Cast on 3 sts, P to end. [22 sts]
* Next row: K1, k2tog, K to end. [21 sts]

* Next row: Cast off 10 sts pwise, P to end. [11 sts]
* Next row: K.
* Next row: Cast off 3 sts pwise, P to end. [8 sts]
* Next row: K1, k2tog, K to end. [7 sts]
* Next row: P.
* Work 4 rows in st st, beg with a K row.
* Next row: Cast on 3 sts, K to end. [10 sts]
* Next row: P.
* Next row: K to last st, m1, K1. [11 sts]
* Work 2 rows in st st, beg with a P row.
* Next row: (p2tog) twice, P to end. [9 sts]
* Next row: Cast off 3 sts, K2 (3 sts on needle incl st rem from casting off), ssk, K1. [5 sts]
* Cast off pwise.

Side 2
Make 1
* Cast on 6 sts in flecked grey.
* 1st row: inc1, K3, inc1, K1. [8 sts]
* Next row: P.
* Next row: (inc1) twice, K to last 3 sts, (inc1) twice, K1. [12 sts]
* Next row: P.
* Rep last 2 rows once more. [16 sts]
* Work 2 rows in st st, beg with a K row.
* Next row: inc1, K to end. [17 sts]
* Next row: P.
* Rep last 2 rows twice more. [19 sts]
* Next row: Cast on 3 sts, K to last 3 sts, ssk, K1. [21 sts]
* Next row: P.
* Next row: Cast off 10 sts, K to end. [11 sts]
* Next row: P.
* Next row: Cast off 3 sts, K to end. [8 sts]
* Next row: P1, p2tog, P to end. [7 sts]
* Work 5 rows in st st, beg with a K row.
* Next row: Cast on 3 sts, P to end. [10 sts]
* Next row: K1, m1, K to end. [11 sts]
* Work 3 rows in st st, beg with a P row.
* Next row: (k2tog) twice, K to end. [9 sts]
* Next row: Cast off 3 sts pwise, P2 (3 sts on needle incl st rem from casting off), p2tog, P1. [5 sts]
* Cast off.

Wings

Right wing
Make 1
* Cast on 7 sts in mid-grey.
* 1st row: inc1, K4, ssk. [7 sts]
* Next and every ws row unless stated: P.
* Next rs row: inc1, K to end. [8 sts]
* Work 7 rows in st st, beg with a P row.
* Next rs row: K1, k2tog, K5. [7 sts]
* Next rs row: K1, (k2tog) twice, K2. [5 sts]
* Next rs row: K1, k2tog, K2. [4 sts]
* Next rs row: k2tog, ssk. [2 sts]
* Next row: p2tog, break yarn and pull it through rem st.

Left wing
Make 1
* Cast on 7 sts in mid-grey.
* 1st row: K1, k2tog, K2, inc1, K1. [7 sts]
* Next and every ws row unless stated: P.
* Next rs row: K5, inc1, K1. [8 sts]
* Work 7 rows in st st, beg with a P row.
* Next rs row: K5, ssk, K1. [7 sts]
* Next rs row: K2, (ssk) twice, K1. [5 sts]
* Next rs row: K2, ssk, K1. [4 sts]
* Next rs row: ssk, k2tog. [2 sts]
* Next row: p2tog, break yarn and pull it through rem st.

Feet
Make 2
* Cast on 5 sts in orange.
* 1st row: Cast off 2 sts, K to end. [3 sts]
* Next row: K1, (inc1) twice. [5 sts]
* Rep last 2 rows once more. [5 sts]
* Cast off.

Beak

The beak is knitted onto the front of the head of the goose, once the two sides of the head have been seamed together.

* Lay the two goose pieces right sides together and sew part of the way down the seam that will lie at the top of the head (you can finish the seam later). Open the piece out.
* Using bright orange yarn, pick up and K 10 sts across the flat front section of the head.
* 1st row: P.
* Next row: K1, k2tog, K4, ssk, K1. [8 sts]
* Next row: p2tog, P4, p2tog. [6 sts]
* Next row: k2tog, K2, ssk. [4 sts]
* Next row: (p2tog) twice. [2 sts]
* Next row: k2tog, break yarn and pull it through rem st.

Making up & finishing

Finish seaming the two sides of the goose together, leaving a gap along the bottom for stuffing. Oversew the curved sections from the inside and use mattress stitch for the straight sections. Stuff the goose and stitch the gap closed.

Oversew the feet to the underside of the goose.

Secure the wings by oversewing around the curved parts where the wings join the body – the ends of the wings should be free.

Using black yarn, work two French knots for the eyes. Using cream yarn, work a circle of chain stitch around the eyes. Split a short length of black yarn lengthways into two thinner lengths. Use one of these to work three straight stitches above each eye for the eyelashes.

On the seventh day of Christmas,
my true love gave to me

Seven swans a-swimming

Six geese a-laying

Five gold rings

Four calling birds

Three French hens

Two turtle doves

And a partridge in a pear tree

Seven swans a-swimming

Swans have long been associated with royalty and royal banquets, so the recipient of all the gifts in this Christmas song was clearly a well-connected lady – although it would have to be some feast for diners to get through all seven swans. And by now, she was probably keen for something more than meat and pet birds to keep her happy. What better gift could there be than a pocket-sized knitted swan?

Equipment
* **A pair of size 3 mm (US 2/3) knitting needles**
* **A pair of size 2.25 mm (US 1) knitting needles**
* **A needle to sew your work together**
* **An embroidery needle**

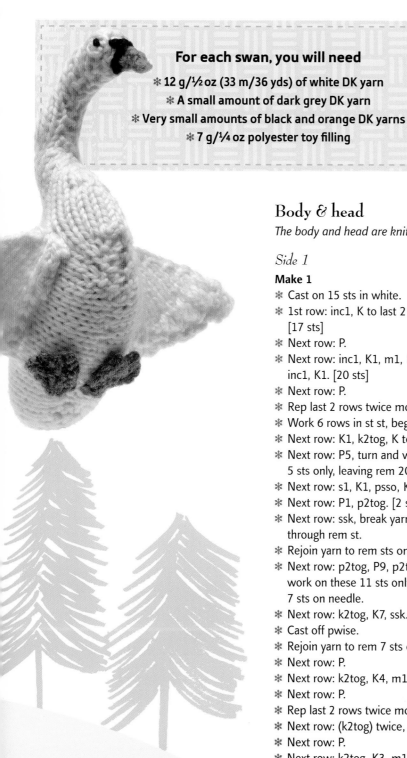

For each swan, you will need
* **12 g/½ oz (33 m/36 yds) of white DK yarn**
* **A small amount of dark grey DK yarn**
* **Very small amounts of black and orange DK yarns**
* **7 g/¼ oz polyester toy filling**

Body & head
The body and head are knitted as one piece.

Side 1
Make 1
* Cast on 15 sts in white.
* 1st row: inc1, K to last 2 sts, inc1, K1. [17 sts]
* Next row: P.
* Next row: inc1, K1, m1, K to last 2 sts, inc1, K1. [20 sts]
* Next row: P.
* Rep last 2 rows twice more. [26 sts]
* Work 6 rows in st st, beg with a K row.
* Next row: K1, k2tog, K to end. [25 sts]
* Next row: P5, turn and work on these 5 sts only, leaving rem 20 sts on needle.
* Next row: s1, K1, psso, K1, ssk. [3 sts]
* Next row: P1, p2tog. [2 sts]
* Next row: ssk, break yarn and pull yarn through rem st.
* Rejoin yarn to rem sts on ws of work.
* Next row: p2tog, P9, p2tog, turn and work on these 11 sts only, leaving rem 7 sts on needle.
* Next row: k2tog, K7, ssk. [9 sts]
* Cast off pwise.
* Rejoin yarn to rem 7 sts on ws of work.
* Next row: P.
* Next row: k2tog, K4, m1, K1. [7 sts]
* Next row: P.
* Rep last 2 rows twice more. [7 sts]
* Next row: (k2tog) twice, K2, m1, K1. [6 sts]
* Next row: P.
* Next row: k2tog, K3, m1, K1. [6 sts]

* Next row: P.
* Next row: inc1, K2, s1, K1, psso, K1. [6 sts]
* Next row: P to last 2 sts, p2tog. [5 sts]
* Next row: inc1, K2, s1, K1, psso. [5 sts]
* Next row: P.
* Rep last 2 rows twice more. [5 sts]
* Next row: Cast on 2 sts, k2tog, K3, s1, K1, psso. [5 sts]
* Work 2 rows in st st, beg with a P row.
* Next row: p2tog, P1, s1 pwise, P1, psso. [3 sts]
* Next row: s1, k2tog, psso, break yarn and pull yarn through rem st.

Side 2
Make 1
* Cast on 15 sts in white.
* 1st row: inc1, K to last 2 sts, inc1, K1. [17 sts]
* Next row: P.
* Next row: inc1, K to last 2 sts, inc1, m1, K1. [20 sts]
* Next row: P.
* Rep last 2 rows twice more. [26 sts]
* Work 6 rows in st st, beg with a K row.
* Next row: K to last 3 sts, s1, K1, psso, K1. [25 sts]
* Next row: P.
* Next row: K5, turn and work on these 5 sts only, leaving rem 20 sts on needle.
* Next row: p2tog, P1, s1 pwise, P1, psso. [3 sts]
* Next row: k2tog, K1. [2 sts]
* Next row: p2tog, break yarn and pull yarn through rem st.
* Rejoin yarn to rem sts on rs of work.

* Next row: k2tog, K9, ssk, turn and work on these 11 sts only, leaving rem 7 sts on needle.
* Next row: p2tog, P7, s1 pwise, P1, psso. [9 sts]
* Cast off.
* Rejoin yarn to rem 7 sts on rs of work.
* Next row: inc1, K4, ssk. [7 sts]
* Next row: P.
* Rep last 2 rows twice more. [7 sts]
* Next row: inc1, K2, (ssk) twice. [6 sts]
* Next row: P.
* Next row: inc1, K3, ssk. [6 sts]
* Next row: P.
* Next row: k2tog, K3, m1, K1. [6 sts]
* Next row: p2tog, P4. [5 sts]
* Next row: k2tog, K2, m1, K1. [5 sts]
* Next row: P.
* Rep last 2 rows twice more.
* Next row: K.
* Next row: Cast on 2 sts, p2tog, P3, p2tog. [5 sts]
* Work 2 rows in st st, beg with a K row.
* Next row: k2tog, K1, ssk. [3 sts]
* Next row: s1 pwise, p2tog, psso, break yarn and pull yarn through rem st.

Beak

Make 1

* Cast on 4 sts in orange, using size 2.25 (US 1) needles.
* 1st row: K.
* Next row: p2tog, s1 pwise, P1, psso. [2 sts]
* Next row: k2tog, break yarn and pull yarn through rem st.

Wings

Right wing

Make 1

* Cast on 6 sts in white.
* 1st row: inc1, K to end. [7 sts]
* Next row: P.
* Rep these 2 rows 5 times more. [12 sts]
* Next row: K1, (yf, k2tog) 5 times, K1. [12 sts]
* Next row: p2tog, P to end. [11 sts]
* Next row: K1, (yf, k2tog) 5 times. [11 sts]
* Next row: p2tog, P to end. [10 sts]
* Next row: K1, (yf, k2tog) 4 times, K1. [10 sts]
* Next row: p2tog, P to end. [9 sts]
* Next row: k2tog then cast off pwise very loosely.

Left wing

Make 1

* Cast on 6 sts in white.
* 1st row: K to last 2 sts, inc1, K1. [7 sts]
* Next row: P.
* Rep these 2 rows 5 times more. [12 sts]
* Next row: K1, (yf, k2tog) 5 times, K1. [12 sts]
* Next row: P to last 2 sts, p2tog. [11 sts]
* Next row: K1, (yf, k2tog) 5 times. [11 sts]
* Next row: P to last 2 sts, p2tog. [10 sts]
* Next row: K1, (yf, k2tog) 4 times, K1. [10 sts]
* Next row: P to last 2 sts, p2tog. [9 sts]
* Next row: k2tog then cast off pwise very loosely.

Feet

Make 2

* Cast on 6 sts in dark grey.
* 1st row: Cast off 2 sts, K to end. [4 sts]
* Next row: K2, (inc1) twice. [6 sts]
* Rep last 2 rows once more.
* Cast off.

Making up & finishing

Seam the two sides of the swan together, leaving a gap along the bottom for stuffing. Oversew the curved sections from the inside and use mattress stitch for the straight sections. Stuff the swan and stitch the gap closed.

Fold the beak piece in half lengthways and oversew around the edges to secure. Stitch the beak in place on the front of the swan's face.

Oversew the feet to the underside of the swan.

Secure the wings by oversewing the wing around the lower edge, the short side edge and the first part of the top edge. Most of the top edge and all of the lacy edge of the wings should be free.

Separate a length of black yarn into two thinner strands. Using one of these, work two French knots for the eyes. Use a separated strand of white yarn to work a circle of small chain stitch around the eyes. Using a separated strand of black yarn, work a ring of chain stitch around the beak, adding a single chain stitch either side of the swan's beak.

On the eighth day of Christmas,

my true love gave to me

Eight maids a-milking

Seven swans a-swimming

Six geese a-laying

Five gold rings

Four calling birds

Three French hens

Two turtle doves

And a partridge in a pear tree

Eight maids a-milking

From this moment on, the gifts get truly extravagant. Before refrigerators were invented, milk was a precious drink because it was impossible to keep it fresh for very long. So the gift of a troupe of milkmaids – and, presumably, the cow and land to go with them – was most generous indeed. Less generous, perhaps, but equally prized are these little woolly maids in their fresh-as-a-daisy outfits.

Equipment

* A pair of size 3 mm (US 2/3) knitting needles
* A 3.25 mm (US D-3) crochet hook
* A needle to sew your work together
* An embroidery needle
* A red crayon

For each maid, you will need

* 8 g/¼ oz (22 m/24 yds) flesh DK yarn
* 5 g/⅛–¼ oz (15 m/16 yds) white DK yarn
* 6 g/¼ oz (18 m/20 yds) light blue DK yarn
* Small amounts of dark brown, dark blue and yellow DK yarns
* Very small amounts of black and red DK yarns
* 20 g/¾ oz polyester toy filling

Body & head

The body and head are knitted as one piece, from the lower edge of the body to the top of the head.

Front
Make 1
* Cast on 16 sts in white.
* Work 7 rows in st st, beg with a K row.
* Next row: K.
* Break yarn and join light blue yarn.
* Next row: K2, (k2tog) twice, K4, (ssk) twice, K2. [12 sts]
* Next row: p2tog, P8, p2tog. [10 sts]
* Next row: K2, m1, K1, m1, K4, m1, K1, m1, K2. [14 sts]
* Next row: P.
* Next row: K2, m1, K10, m1, K2. [16 sts]
* Work 8 rows in st st, beg with a P row.
* Next row: K.
* Break yarn and join flesh yarn.
* Work 2 rows in st st, beg with a K row.
* Next row: K2, k2tog, K8, ssk, K2. [14 sts]
* Next row: P.
* Next row: K2, k2tog, K6, ssk, K2. [12 sts]
* Next row: P.
* Next row: K2, m1, K1, m1, K6, m1, K1, m1, K2. [16 sts]
* Next row: P.*
* Work 8 rows in st st, beg with a K row.
* Next row: K2, k2tog, K to last 4 sts, ssk, K2. [14 sts]

* Next row: p2tog, P to last 2 sts, p2tog. [12 sts]
* Rep last 2 rows once more. [8 sts]
* Cast off.

Back
Make 1
* Work as for front as far as *.
* Break yarn and join yellow yarn.
* Work 8 rows in st st, beg with a K row.
* Next row: K2, k2tog, K to last 4 sts, ssk, K2. [14 sts]
* Next row: p2tog, P to last 2 sts, p2tog. [12 sts]
* Rep last 2 rows once more. [8 sts]
* Cast off.

Arms

The arms are knitted from the top of the arm to the tip of the hand.

Make 2
* Cast on 7 sts in light blue.
* Work 9 rows in st st, beg with a K row.
* Next row: K.
* Break yarn and join flesh yarn.
* Work 18 rows in st st, beg with a K row.
* Next row: K1, k2tog, K1, ssk, K1. [5 sts]
* Cast off pwise.

Boots & legs

The boots and legs are made as one piece and are knitted from the sole of the boot to the top of the leg.

Make 2
* Cast on 28 sts in dark brown.
* Work 4 rows in st st, beg with a K row.
* Next row: K5, cast off 18 sts, K to end. [10 sts]
* Work 6 rows in st st, beg with a P row.
* Next row: K.
* Break yarn and join flesh yarn.
* Work 18 rows in st st, beg with a K row.
* Cast off.

Skirt

Make 2 pieces
* Cast on 24 sts in light blue.
* Work 3 rows in st st, beg with a P row.
* Leave light blue yarn at the side but do not break.
* Join dark blue yarn and K 2 rows. Break yarn.
* Pick up light blue yarn and work 14 rows in st st, beg with a K row.
* Next row: (k2tog, K1) 4 times, (K1, ssk) 4 times. [16 sts]
* Cast off pwise.

Apron

The apron is knitted from the lower edge to the top edge.

Make 1
* Cast on 16 sts in white.
* 1st row: K.
* Next row: K1, (yf, k2tog) 7 times, K1.
* Next row: K.
* Next row: K.
* Next row: K2, P to last 2 sts, K2.
* Rep last 2 rows 4 times more.
* Next row: (k2tog) 4 times, (ssk) 4 times. [8 sts]
* Cast off kwise, leaving a long yarn tail.

Cap

* Cast on 12 sts in white.
* K 2 rows.
* Work 6 rows in st st, beg with a K row.
* Next row: Cast on 4 sts, K to end. [16 sts]
* Next row: Cast on 4 sts, K2, P to last 2 sts, K2. [20 sts]
* Next row: K.
* Next row: K2, P to last 2 sts, K2.
* Rep last 2 rows twice more.
* Next row: K1, (yf, k2tog) 9 times, K1.
* Next row: K.
* Cast off.

Making up & finishing

Oversew the side and top seams of the head with the pieces right sides together. Turn the right way out and join the side seams. Stuff through the lower edge and close the gap.

Using black yarn, work two French knots for the eyes. Using white yarn, work a circle of chain stitch around the eyes. Use a single strand of black yarn to work three straight stitches for the eyelashes.

Using red yarn, work two straight stitches in a V shape for the mouth. For the nose, work a small circle of chain stitch in flesh yarn. Use a red crayon to colour the cheeks.

For the hair, make two 12-cm (5-in) crochet chains in yellow. Embroider a few rows of chain stitch on each side of the head. Fold each crochet chain into two loops and fasten at the side of the head.

Fold the leg pieces in half lengthways, right sides together. Oversew the top and base of the boots. Turn the pieces right side out and sew the back seams of the boot and leg using mattress stitch. Stuff the legs.

Fold the arm pieces in half lengthways, right sides together. Oversew around the hands. Turn the pieces right side out and join the side seam using mattress stitch. The arms do not need stuffing.

Sew the legs to the outer edge of the lower edge of the body. Sew the arms to the side of the body, with the tops about 5 mm (¼ in) above the dress neckline.

With right sides of the skirt pieces together, oversew the side seams using mattress stitch. Oversew the waist edge of the skirt to the bodice.

Using the yarn tail at the waist edge of the apron, work a 10-cm (4-in) crochet chain for one of the apron ties. Make a matching chain and fasten it to the other side.

Fold the sides of the cap inwards with the right sides facing in. Oversew the side seams.

Fold up the front edge of the cap to form a picot edge (see page 15) and oversew in place. Oversew the cap on the doll's head.

Using black yarn, work a few straight stitches on the boots and tie the yarn tails in small bows at the ankles.

On the ninth day of Christmas, my true love gave to me

Nine ladies dancing

Eight maids a-milking

Seven swans a-swimming

Six geese a-laying

Five gold rings

Four calling birds

Three French hens

Two turtle doves

And a partridge in a pear tree

Nine ladies dancing

Waltzes, polkas and pirouettes: you name it, some ladies are just born to dance! With their trim figures, flouncy skirts and pastel dancing slippers, these ladies are ready to catch the eye of a passing gent and dance the night away at the Christmas season party.

Equipment

* A pair of size 3 mm (US 2/3) knitting needles
* A 3.25 mm (US D-3) crochet hook
* A needle to sew your work together
* An embroidery needle
* A red crayon

For each lady, you will need

* 10 g/⅜ oz (28 m/31 yds) cream DK yarn
* 20 g/¾ oz (44 m/48 yds) pale pink DK yarn
* Small amounts of pale turquoise and mid-brown DK yarns
* Very small amounts of black and deep pink DK yarns
* A small bright pink button
* Black sewing thread
* 20 g (¾ oz) polyester toy filling

Body & head

The body and head are knitted as one piece, from the lower edge of the body to the top of the head.

Front

Make 1

* Cast on 14 sts in pale pink.
* Work 8 rows in st st, beg with a K row.
* Next row: K2, (k2tog) twice, K2, (ssk) twice, K2. [10 sts]
* Next row: p2tog, P6, p2tog. [8 sts]
* Next row: K2, m1, K1, m1, K2, m1, K1, m1, K2. [12 sts]
* Next row: P.
* Next row: K2, m1, K8, m1, K2. [14 sts]
* Work 8 rows in st st, beg with a P row.
* Next row: K.
* Break yarn and join cream yarn.
* Work 2 rows in st st, beg with a K row.
* Next row: K2, k2tog, K to last 4 sts, ssk, K2. [12 sts]
* Next row: P.
* Rep last 2 rows once more. [10 sts]
* Next row: K2, m1, K1, m1, K4, m1, K1, m1, K2. [14 sts]
* Next row: P.*
* Work 10 rows in st st, beg with a K row.
* Next row: K2, k2tog, K to last 4 sts, ssk, K2. [12 sts]
* Next row: p2tog, P to last 2 sts, p2tog. [10 sts]
* Rep last 2 rows once more. [6 sts]
* Cast off.

Back

Make 1

* Work as for front as far as *.
* Break yarn and join brown yarn.
* Work 10 rows in st st, beg with a K row.
* Next row: K2, k2tog, K to last 4 sts, ssk, K2. [12 sts]
* Next row: p2tog, P to last 2 sts, p2tog. [10 sts]
* Rep last 2 rows once more. [6 sts]
* Cast off.

Arms

The arms are knitted from the top of the arm to the tip of the hand.

Make 2

* Cast on 7 sts in pale pink.
* Work 9 rows in st st, beg with a K row.
* Next row: K.
* Break yarn and join cream yarn.
* Work 18 rows in st st, beg with a K row.
* Next row: K1, k2tog, K1, ssk, K1. [5 sts]
* Cast off pwise.

Nose

* Using your crochet hook, make a 3-cm (1¼-in) crochet chain in cream yarn.

Feet & legs

The feet and legs are made as one piece and are knitted from the sole of the foot to the top of the leg. The shoes are knitted separately.

Make 2
✳ Cast on 28 sts in cream.
✳ Work 4 rows in st st, beg with a K row.
✳ Next row: K5, cast off 18 sts, K to end. [10 sts]
✳ Work 25 rows in st st, beg with a P row.
✳ Cast off.

Skirt

The skirt is knitted in a simple lace stitch. The right side of your work is the side where you work the plain knit row. The reverse side of your work is where you take your yarn to the front of your work and then knit two stitches together.

Make 2 pieces
✳ Cast on 22 sts in pale pink.
✳ 1st row: K.
✳ Next row: K1, (yf, k2tog) to last st, K1.
✳ Rep last 2 rows 3 times more.
✳ Next row: K1, k2tog, K to last 3 sts, ssk, K1. [20 sts]
✳ Next row: K2, (yf, k2tog) to end.
✳ Next row: K.
✳ Next row: K2, (yf, k2tog) to end.
✳ Rep last 2 rows twice more.
✳ Next row: K1, k2tog, K to last 3 sts, ssk, K1. [18 sts]
✳ Next row: K1, (yf, k2tog) to last st, K1.
✳ Next row: K.
✳ Next row: K1, (yf, k2tog) to last st, K1.
✳ Rep last 2 rows twice more.
✳ Next row: K1, k2tog, K to last 3 sts, ssk, K1. [16 sts]
✳ Next row: K2, (yf, k2tog) to end.
✳ Next row: K.
✳ Next row: K2, (yf, k2tog) to end.
✳ Rep last 2 rows twice more.
✳ Next row: K1, k2tog, K to last 3 sts, ssk, K1. [14 sts]
✳ Next row: K1, (yf, k2tog) to last st, K1.
✳ Next row: K.
✳ Next row: K2, (yf, k2tog) to end.
✳ Rep last 2 rows twice more.
✳ Next row: K.
✳ Cast off.

Dancing slippers

Make 2
✳ Cast on 6 sts in pale turquoise.
✳ 1st row: inc1, K3, inc1, K1. [8 sts]
✳ Next row: P.
✳ Next row: K1, m1, K6, m1, K1. [10 sts]
✳ Work 5 rows in st st, beg with a P row.
✳ Next row: K5, turn and work on these sts only, leaving rem 5 sts on needle.
✳ Work 9 rows in st st, beg with a P row.
✳ Cast off.
✳ Rejoin yarn to sts on needle on rs of work.
✳ Work 10 rows in st st, beg with a K row.
✳ Cast off.

Making up & finishing

With the body and head pieces right sides together, oversew the side and top seams of the head. Turn the pieces right side out and join the side seams of the body using mattress stitch, leaving the bottom edge open. Stuff and then close the gap using mattress stitch.

Fold the leg pieces in half lengthways, right sides together. Oversew the top and base of the feet. Turn the pieces right side out and sew the back seams of the feet and leg using mattress stitch. Stuff the legs fairly firmly.

Fold the arm pieces in half lengthways, right sides together. Oversew around the hand. Turn the pieces right side out and join the side seam using mattress stitch. The arms do not need stuffing.

Sew the legs to the outer edge of the lower edge of the body. Sew the arms to the side of the body, with the tops about 5 mm (¼ in) above the dress neckline.

Using black yarn, work two French knots for the eyes. Using cream yarn, work a circle of chain stitch around the eyes. Use a single strand of black to work three straight stitches at the top of each eye for the eyelashes.

Fold the cream crochet chain for the nose in half widthways and sew it to the face with matching yarn. Using deep pink yarn, work two straight stitches, one on top of the other, for the mouth. Use a red crayon to colour the cheeks.

For the hair, embroider a few rows of chain stitch in brown yarn on each side of the head. For the bun, wind brown yarn about 12 times around a pencil. Remove the coil and attach to the top of the head with a few stitches.

With right sides together, oversew the skirt side seams. The skirt will twist around slightly at the bottom, which gives a nice flared look. Oversew the waist edge of the skirt to the bodice. Using black sewing thread, sew the button to the front of the skirt.

Join the lower and back seams of the dancing slippers. Oversew the shoes in place on the doll and add a large cross stitch across the top of each foot to represent ribbon ties.

On the tenth day of Christmas, my true love gave to me

Ten lords a-leaping

Nine ladies dancing

Eight maids a-milking

Seven swans a-swimming

Six geese a-laying

Five gold rings

Four calling birds

Three French hens

Two turtle doves

And a partridge in a pear tree

***

Ten lords a-leaping

These fit-as-a-fiddle gents enjoy nothing more than showing off their physical prowess. Dressed in their finest cloaks and hats, their job is to entertain guests between courses in high-society homes during the pre-Christmas celebrations and to ensure that a good time is had by all.

Equipment
* A pair of size 3 mm (US 2/3) knitting needles
* A 3.25 mm (US D-3) crochet hook
* A needle to sew your work together
* An embroidery needle

For each lord, you will need
* 3 g/⅛ oz (7 m/8 yds) cream DK yarn
* 8 g/¼ oz (21 m/23 yds) dark red DK yarn
* 6 g/¼ oz (16 m/18 yds) of yellow DK yarn
* 4 g/⅛ oz (11 m/12 yds) of black DK yarn
* Small amounts of purple and orange DK yarns
* A small amount of white mohair yarn
* A very small amount of bright red DK yarn
* A very small amount of gold crochet yarn
* Three small white buttons
* Black sewing thread
* 20 g (¾ oz) polyester toy filling

Body & head
The body and head are knitted as one piece, from the lower edge of the body to the top of the head.

Make 2
* Cast on 14 sts in black.
* Work 6 rows in st st, beg with a K row.
* Break yarn and join yellow yarn for pullover.
* K 4 rows.
* Work 12 rows in st st, beg with a K row.
* Next row: K2, k2tog, K6, ssk, K2. [12 sts]
* Next row: P.
* Next row: K2, k2tog, K4, ssk, K2. [10 sts]
* K 3 rows.
* Break yarn and join cream yarn for face.
* Work 2 rows in st st, beg with a K row.
* Next row: K2, m1, K1, m1, K4, m1, K1, m1, K2. [14 sts]
* Work 9 rows in st st, beg with a P row.
* Break yarn and join orange yarn for hat.
* Work 2 rows in st st, beg with a K row.
* Next row: K2, k2tog, K to last 4 sts, ssk, K2. [12 sts]
* Next row: p2tog, P to last 2 sts, p2tog. [10 sts]
* Rep last 2 rows once more. [6 sts]
* Cast off.

Arms
The arms are knitted from the top of the arm to the tip of the hand.

Make 2
* Cast on 7 sts in yellow.
* Work 24 rows in st st, beg with a K row.
* K 4 rows.
* Break yarn and join cream yarn for hands.
* Work 4 rows in st st, beg with a K row.
* Next row: K1, k2tog, K1, ssk, K1. [5 sts]
* Cast off pwise.

Boots & legs

The boots and legs are made as one piece and are knitted from the boot to the top of the leg.

Make 2
* Cast on 28 sts in purple.
* Work 4 rows in st st, beg with a K row.
* Next row: K5, cast off 18 sts, K to end. [10 sts]
* Next row: P.
* Break yarn and join black yarn for trousers.
* K 2 rows.
* Work 24 rows in st st, beg with a K row.
* Cast off.

Hat brim

Make 1
* Cast on 24 sts in orange.
* 1st row: K.
* Work 4 rows in st st, beg with a K row.
* Next row: K2, (yf, k2tog) 10 times, K2. [24 sts]
* Work 3 rows in st st, beg with a P row.
* Cast off loosely.

Cloak

The cloak starts off as three separate pieces.

Part 1

Make 1
* Cast on 5 sts in dark red.
* Work 2 rows in st st, beg with a K row.
* Next row: K2, m1, K3. [6 sts]
* Next row: K1, P5.
* Next row: K.
* Next row: K1, P5.
* Next row: K2, m1, K4. [7 sts]
* Next row: K1, P6.
* Break yarn and leave sts on needle. Cast on the next section of the cloak on the needle where you have left the sts.

Part 2

Make 1
* Cast on 12 sts in dark red.
* Work 2 rows in st st, beg with a K row.
* Next row: K2, m1, K to last 2 sts, m1, K2. [14 sts]
* Work 3 rows in st st, beg with a P row.
* Next row: K2, m1, K to last 2 sts, m1, K2. [16 sts]
* Next row: P.
* Break yarn and leave sts on needle. Cast on the next section of the cloak on the needle where you have left the sts.

Part 3

Make 1
* Cast on 5 sts in dark red.
* Work 2 rows in st st, beg with a K row.
* Next row: K3, m1, K2. [6 sts]
* Next row: P5, K1.
* Next row: K.
* Next row: P5, K1.
* Next row: K4, m1, K2. [7 sts]
* Next row: P6, K1.
* Do not break yarn.
You will now have three pieces on your needle.
* Next row: K across 7 sts from third piece, 16 sts from second piece and 7 sts from first piece. [30 sts]
* Next and every ws row: K1, P to last st, K1.
* Next rs row: K6, m1, K2, m1, K14, m1, K2, m1, K6. [34 sts]
* Next rs row: K.
* Next rs row: K7, m1, K2, m1, K16, m1, K2, m1, K7. [38 sts]
* Next rs row: K.
* Next rs row: K8, m1, K2, m1, K18, m1, K2, m1, K8. [42 sts]
* Next rs row: K.
* Next rs row: K9, m1, K2, m1, K20, m1, K2, m1, K9. [46 sts]
* Next rs row: K.
* Next ws row: K1, P to last st, K1.
* Repeat last 2 rows 4 times more.
* Break yarn and join white mohair yarn.
* Work 3 rows in st st, beg with a K row.
* Cast off loosely pwise.
* With the rs of your work facing you and using dark red yarn, pick up and K 5 sts across the top edge of one side piece of cloak, 12 sts across back section and 5 sts across second side piece of cloak. [22 sts]
* K 12 rows.
* Cast off loosely.

Half back belt for cloak

* Cast on 3 sts in dark red.
* K 18 rows.
* Cast off.

Hair

* Using your crochet hook, make two 10-cm (4-in) crochet chains in black yarn.

Nose

* Using your crochet hook, make a 3-cm (1¼-in) crochet chain in cream yarn.

Making up & finishing

With the body and head pieces right sides together, oversew the side and top seams of the hat and head. Turn right side out and join the side seams of the body using mattress stitch, leaving the bottom edge open. Stuff, then close the gap using mattress stitch.

Using black yarn, work two French knots for the eyes. Using cream yarn, work a circle of chain stitch around the eyes. Using bright red yarn, work a straight stitch for the mouth.

Fold the cream crochet chain for the nose in half widthways and sew it to the face with matching yarn.

For the hair, make each black crochet chain into two even loops and join them to the side of the head. Using black yarn, work the moustache in chain stitch.

Fold the leg pieces in half lengthways, right sides together. Oversew the top and base of the boots. Turn the pieces right side out and sew the back seams of the boots and leg using mattress stitch. Stuff the legs.

Fold the arm pieces in half lengthways, right sides together. Oversew around the hands. Turn the pieces right side out and join the side seam using mattress stitch. The arms do not need stuffing.

Sew the legs to the outer edge of the lower edge of the body. Sew the arms to the side of the body, with the tops of the arms 1 cm (³/₈ in) below the pullover neck edge.

Fold the hat brim in half lengthways so that the right side is on the outside and the eyelets form a picot edge (see page 15). Oversew the cast-off edge in place, then join the short edges to form a circle. Oversew the hat brim in place.

Using black sewing thread, attach the back belt about halfway up the back of the cloak by sewing a small button to each side. Sew another button to the front of the cloak, through both layers, to join the two sides of the cloak together. Using black yarn, work a row of running stitches along the mohair trim of the cloak.

For the boot buckles, using gold crochet yarn, work a small square of chain stitch on the top of each boot.

On the eleventh day of Christmas, my true love gave to me

Eleven pipers piping

Eleven pipers piping

Who doesn't want to hear a few rousing melodies during the Christmas season? Bands of pipers attended Christmas feasts to provide the music for the revelries and dancing – and what an amazing gift to be given your own troupe. We can't pretend that these knitted pipers will provide the soundtrack for your Christmas party – but they'll certainly look the part!

Equipment
* A pair of size 3 mm (US 2/3) knitting needles
* A needle to sew your work together
* An embroidery needle
* A red crayon

For each piper, you will need
* 6 g/¼ oz (15 m/16 yds) light beige DK yarn
* 7 g/¼ oz (19 m/21 yds) turquoise DK yarn
* 7 g/¼ oz (20 m/22 yds) red DK yarn
* 4 g/⅛ oz (10 m/11 yds) black DK yarn
* Small amounts of mid-brown and ochre DK yarns
* Very small amounts of white and deep pink DK yarns
* 4 tiny black buttons
* Red sewing thread
* 20 g/¾ oz polyester toy filling

Body & head
The body and head are knitted as one piece, from the lower edge of the body to the top of the head.

Front
* Cast on 14 sts in turquoise.
* Work 6 rows in st st, beg with a K row.
* K 2 rows.
* Break yarn and join light beige yarn for body and head.
* Work 10 rows in st st, beg with a K row.
* Next row: K2, k2tog, K6, ssk, K2. [12 sts]
* Next row: P.
* Next row: K2, k2tog, K4, ssk, K2. [10 sts]
* Work 3 rows in st st, beg with a P row.
* Next row: K2, m1, K1, m1, K4, m1, K1, m1, K2. [14 sts]
* Next row: P.*
* Work 10 rows in st st, beg with a K row.
* Next row: K2, k2tog, K to last 4 sts, ssk, K2. [12 sts]
* Next row: p2tog, P to last 2 sts, p2tog. [10 sts]
* Rep last 2 rows once more. [6 sts]
* Cast off.

Back
* Work as for front as far as *.
* Work 4 rows in st st, beg with a K row.
* Break yarn and join mid-brown yarn for hair.
* Work 6 rows in st st, beg with a K row.
* Next row: K2, k2tog, K to last 4 sts, ssk, K2. [12 sts]
* Next row: p2tog, P to last 2 sts, p2tog. [10 sts]
* Rep last 2 rows once more. [6 sts]
* Cast off.

Arms
The arms are knitted from the top of the arm to the tip of the hand.

Make 2
* Cast on 7 sts in red.
* Work 24 rows in st st, beg with a K row.
* K 4 rows.
* Break yarn and join light beige for hands.
* Work 4 rows in st st, beg with a K row.
* Next row: K1, k2tog, K1, ssk, K1. [5 sts]
* Cast off pwise.

Boots & legs
The boots and legs are made as one piece and are knitted from the boot to the top of the leg.

Make 2
* Cast on 28 sts in black.
* Work 4 rows in st st, beg with a K row.
* Next row: K5, cast off 18 sts, K to end. [10 sts]
* Work 8 rows in st st, beg with a P row.
* Next row: K.
* Break yarn and join turquoise yarn for trousers.
* Work 18 rows in st st, beg with a K row.
* Cast off.

Jacket
The jacket's sleeves are part of the doll. The rest of the jacket is knitted as one piece and then sewn around the sleeves.

Make 1
* Cast on 38 sts in red.
* K 2 rows.
* Next and every ws row: K2, P to last 2 sts, K2.
* Next rs row: K.
* Work 1 ws row.
* Leave red yarn at the side of your work and join turquoise yarn.

* K 2 rows.
* Break turquoise yarn and pick up red yarn.
* Work 8 rows in st st, beg with a K row, remembering to K 2 sts at beg and end of every ws row.
* Next row: K12, turn and work on these sts only, leaving rem sts on needle.
* Next row: P to last 2 sts, K2.
* Next row: K.
* Break yarn and rejoin it to rem sts on rs of work.
* Next row: K14, turn and work on these sts only, leaving rem sts on needle.
* Next row: P.
* Next row: K.
* Break yarn and rejoin it to rem 12 sts on rs of work.
* Next row: K.
* Next row: K2, P to end.
* Next row: K.
* Now knit across all sts on needle as follows:
* Next row: K2, P9, p2tog, P12, p2tog, P9, K2. [36 sts]
* Next row: Cast off 2 sts kwise, K6 (7 sts on needle incl st rem from casting off), k2tog, (K1, k2tog) twice, K2, (ssk, K1) twice, ssk, K to end. [28 sts]
* Next row: Cast off 2 sts, K to end. [26 sts]
* Next row: K.
* Cast off kwise.

Cap

The cap is knitted in two main parts – the side band and the tip. The peak is knitted onto the side band once the two main parts of the cap have been stitched together.

Side band

* Cast on 28 sts in turquoise.
* 1st row: P.
* Next row: (K2, m1) to last 2 sts, K2. [41 sts]
* Work 3 rows in st st, beg with a P row.
* Cast off.

Tip

* Cast on 5 sts in turquoise.
* 1st row: inc1, K3, inc1. [7 sts]
* Next row: P.
* Next row: (inc1) twice, K to last 3 sts, (inc1) twice, K1. [11 sts]
* Next row: P.
* Rep last 2 rows once more. [15 sts]
* Next row: inc1, K12, inc1, K1. [17 sts]
* Work 7 rows in st st, beg with a P row.
* Next row: K1, k2tog, K11, ssk, K1. [15 sts]

* Next row: P.
* Next row: K1, (k2tog) twice, K5, (ssk) twice, K1. [11 sts]
* Next row: P.
* Next row: K1, (k2tog) twice, K1, (ssk) twice, K1. [7 sts]
* Cast off pwise.

Join the short edges of the side band. With the right sides of your work facing you, place the tip on the side band so that your rows of knitting run across the side band. Work a row of running stitch around the tip to join the tip to the side band.

Peak

* Using black yarn, pick up and K 11 sts across front of side band.
* Next row: P.
* Next row: K1, k2tog, K5, ssk, K1. [9 sts]
* Next row: P.
* Next row: K1, k2tog, K3, ssk, K1. [7 sts]
* Next row: p2tog, P3, p2tog. [5 sts]
* Next row: K1, m1, K to last st, m1, K1. [7 sts]
* Next row: P.
* Rep last 2 rows once more. [9 sts]
* Next row: K1, m1, K to last st, m1, K1. [11 sts]
* Cast off pwise.

Fold the cast-off edge of the peak under. Oversew the sides of the peak together and the cast-off edge of the peak to the inside of the side band.

Pipe

* Cast on 8 sts in ochre.
* Work 2 rows in st st, beg with a K row.
* Next row: K1, k2tog, K2, ssk, K1. [6 sts]
* Work 3 rows in st st, beg with a P row.
* Next row: K1, k2tog, ssk, K1. [4 sts]
* Work 7 rows in st st, beg with a P row.
* Cast off.

Making up & finishing

With the two body and head pieces right sides together, oversew the side and top seams of the head. Turn the pieces right side out and join the side seams of the body using mattress stitch, leaving the bottom edge of the body open. Stuff. Close the gap using mattress stitch.

Using black yarn, work two French knots for the eyes. Using white yarn, work a circle of chain stitch around the eyes.

Using deep pink yarn, work two straight stitches, one on top of the other, for the mouth.

Using light beige yarn, embroider two lines of chain stitch for the nose.

Use your red crayon to colour the cheeks.

For the hair, using mid-brown yarn, embroider several rows of chain stitch from one side of the head to the other.

Fold the leg pieces in half lengthways, right sides together. Oversew the top and base of the boots. Turn the pieces the right way out and sew the back seams of the boots and leg using mattress stitch. Stuff the legs fairly firmly.

Fold the arm pieces in half lengthways, right sides together. Oversew around the hand. Turn the pieces right side out and join the side seam using mattress stitch. The arms do not need stuffing.

Sew the legs to the outer edge of the lower edge of the body. Sew the arms to the side of the body, with the tops of the arms about 1 cm (3/8 in) below the top edge of the neck. Using black yarn, work a row of chain stitch down the outer side of each leg.

Put the jacket on the doll and oversew the armhole edges around the top of the arms. Sew the buttons to the left-hand side of the jacket using black sewing thread.

Sew the side seam of the pipe.

On the twelfth day of Christmas,

my true love gave to me

Twelve drummers drumming

Eleven pipers piping
Ten lords a-leaping
Nine ladies dancing
Eight maids a-milking
Seven swans a-swimming
Six geese a-laying
Five gold rings
Four calling birds
Three French hens
Two turtle doves
And a partridge in a pear tree

Twelve drummers drumming

The twelfth day of Christmas marks the end of the build-up to the Christmas season and the night before the Three Wise Men arrived with gifts for the infant Jesus. Just like today, in times gone by, drums were often used in the build-up to the announcement of an important event. And we trust that these woolly drummers will make a big noise – though not in the literal sense, of course!

Equipment

* A pair of size 3 mm (US 2/3) knitting needles
* A 3.25 mm (US D-3) crochet hook
* A needle to sew your work together
* An embroidery needle
* A red crayon

For each drummer, you will need
* 6 g/¼ oz (15 m/16 yds) dark beige DK yarn
* 11 g/¼–½ oz (31 m/34 yds) purple DK yarn
* 4 g/⅛ oz (12 m/13 yds) dark grey DK yarn
* 3 g/⅛ oz (7 m/8 yds) black DK yarn
* 3 g/⅛ oz (8 m/9 yds) red DK yarn
* Small amounts of lime green, yellow, orange and pale grey DK yarns
* Very small amounts of bright pink and white DK yarns
* 20 g/¾ oz polyester toy filling
* A medium-size pale green button
* 4 tiny grey buttons
* Lime green sewing thread
* Two 4-cm (1½-in) lengths of plastic-coated wire

Body & head
The body and head are knitted as one piece, from the lower edge of the body to the top of the head.

Front
Make 1
* Cast on 14 sts in dark grey.
* Work 6 rows in st st, beg with a K row.
* K 2 rows.
* Break yarn and join dark beige yarn.
* Work 10 rows in st st, beg with a K row.
* Next row: K2, k2tog, K6, ssk, K2. [12 sts]
* Next row: P.
* Next row: K2, k2tog, K4, ssk, K2. [10 sts]
* Work 3 rows in st st, beg with a P row.
* Next row: K2, m1, K1, m1, K4, m1, K1, m1, K2. [14 sts]
* Next row: P.*
* Work 10 rows in st st, beg with a K row.
* Next row: K2, k2tog, K to last 4 sts, ssk, K2. [12 sts]
* Next row: p2tog, P to last 2 sts, p2tog. [10 sts]
* Rep last 2 rows once more. [6 sts]
* Cast off.

Back
Make 1
* Work as for front as far as *.
* Work 4 rows in st st, beg with a K row.
* Break yarn and join black yarn for hair.
* Work 6 rows in st st, beg with a K row.
* Next row: K2, k2tog, K to last 4 sts, ssk, K2. [12 sts]
* Next row: p2tog, P to last 2 sts, p2tog. [10 sts]
* Rep last 2 rows once more. [6 sts]
* Cast off.

Arms
The arms are knitted from the top of the arm to the tip of the hand.

Make 2
* Cast on 7 sts in purple.
* Work 24 rows in st st, beg with a K row.
* K 4 rows.
* Break yarn and join dark beige yarn for hands.
* Work 4 rows in st st, beg with a K row.
* Next row: K1, k2tog, K1, ssk, K1. [5 sts]
* Cast off pwise.

Boots & legs

Make 2
* Cast on 28 sts in black.
* Work 4 rows in st st.
* Next row: K5, cast off 18 sts, K to end. [10 sts]
* Next row: P.
* Break yarn and join dark grey for trousers.
* K 2 rows.
* Work 2 rows in st st, beg with a K row.
* K 2 rows.
* Work 20 rows in st st, beg with a K row.
* Cast off.

Jacket

Make 1
* Cast on 38 sts in purple.
* K 2 rows.
* Next and every ws row: K2, P to last 2 sts, K2.
* Work 19 rows in st st, beg with a K row, remembering to K 2 sts at beg and end of every ws row.
* Next row: K12, turn and work on these sts only, leaving rem sts on needle.
* Next row: P to last 2 sts, K2.
* Next row: K.
* Break yarn and rejoin it to rem sts on rs of work.
* Next row: K14, turn and work on these sts only, leaving rem sts on needle.
* Next row: P.
* Next row: K.
* Break yarn and rejoin it to rem 12 sts on rs of work.
* Next row: K
* Next row: K2, P to end.
* Next row: K.
* Now knit across all sts on needle as follows:
* Next row: Cast off 3 sts kwise, K8 (9 sts on needle incl st rem from casting off), k2tog, K1, k2tog, K4, ssk, K1, ssk, K to end. [31 sts]
* Next row: Cast off 3 sts, K to end. [28 sts]
* K 3 rows.
* Cast off.
* For the belt, cast on 30 sts in lime green. Cast off.

Hat

Make 1
* Cast on 28 sts in purple.
* K 2 rows.
* Next row: P.

* Next row: K2, (m1, K3) 8 times, m1, K2. [37 sts]
* Work 5 rows in st st, beg with a P row.
* Next row: Cast off 16 sts, K to end. [21 sts]
* Next row: Cast off 16 sts pwise, P to end. [5 sts]
* Next row: K1, m1, inc1, K1, inc1, m1, K1. [9 sts]
* Next row: P.
* Next row: K1, m1, K to last st, m1, K1. [11 sts]
* Next row: P.
* Rep last 2 rows twice more. [15 sts]
* Next row: K1, k2tog, K to last 3 sts, ssk, K1. [13 sts]
* Next row: P.
* Rep last 2 rows twice more. [9 sts]
* Next row: K1, k2tog, K3, ssk, K1. [7 sts]
* Cast off pwise.

Drum

Shell

Make 1
* Cast on 28 sts in red.
* K 2 rows.
* Next row: P.
* K 2 rows.
* Cast off.

Heads

Make 2
* Cast on 3 sts in red.
* 1st row: (inc1) twice, K1. [5 sts]
* Next row: inc1, K to last 2 sts, inc1, K1. [7 sts]
* Next row: P.
* Rep last 2 rows twice more. [11 sts]
* Work 2 rows in st st, beg with a K row.
* Next row: K1, k2tog, K to last 3 sts, ssk, K1. [9 sts]
* Next row: P.
* Rep last 2 rows once more. [7 sts]
* Next row: K1, k2tog, K1, ssk, K1. [5 sts]
* Cast off pwise.

Hoops
* Using your crochet hook, make two 11.5-cm (4½-in) crochet chains in yellow yarn.

Cord
* Using your crochet hook, make a 16-cm (6¼-in) crochet chain in orange yarn.

Drumsticks
* Cast on 11 sts in pale grey.
* Cast off.

Making up & finishing

Oversew the side and top seams of the head with the pieces right sides together. Turn the right way out and join the side seams. Stuff through the lower edge and close the gap.

Using black yarn, work two French knots for the eyes. Using white yarn, work a circle of chain stitch around the eyes. Work a V shape for the mouth in red yarn and embroider the nose in chain stitch using dark beige yarn. Use a red crayon to colour the cheeks.

Using black yarn, embroider a few rows of chain stitch for the hair.

Fold the leg pieces in half lengthways, right sides together. Oversew the top and base of the boots. Turn right side out and sew the back seams using mattress stitch. Stuff.

Fold the arm pieces in half lengthways, right sides together. Oversew around the hand. Turn right side out and join the side seam. Do not stuff.

Sew the legs and arms to the body. Using lime green yarn, work a row of chain stitch down the outer side of each leg and around the end of each sleeve.

Oversew the armhole edges of the jacket around the tops of the arms. Sew on the buttons. Join the short edges of the belt.

Join the back seam of the hat and join the shaped edges of the hat crown to the sides. Sew on three small loops of bright pink yarn and the green button.

Seam the drum pieces together leaving a small gap. Stuff then close the gap.

Sew the hoops in place and work some V-shaped yellow stitches around the shell. Fasten the cord to the drum. Oversew the sides of the drumstick pieces together, around the lengths of wire.

Index